...OH GOOD
iT'S **YOU** AGAIN!!
i WASN'T LOOKING FORWARD
TO CONTINUING
THROUGH LiFE
ALONE!!

More Humor by Tom Wilson From SIGNET

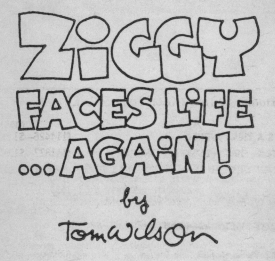

by
Tom Wilson

A SIGNET BOOK
NEW AMERICAN LIBRARY
TIMES MIRROR

Published by arrangement with Andrews and McMeel, Inc.,
a Universal Press Syndicate Company

ZIGGY FACES LIFE was originally published by Andrews & McMeel, Inc.,
as a 128-page large-format paperback. The Signet edition ZIGGY
FACES LIFE comprises the first half of the book, and ZIGGY FACES
LIFE . . . AGAIN! the second half.

First Signet Printing, September, 1982

5 6 7 8 9

PRINTED IN THE UNITED STATES OF AMERICA

EVERYONE SAYS ANTS ARE SO INDUSTRIOUS....
... HOW DO WE KNOW IF MAYBE THEY ONLY ACT BUSY WHEN SOMEBODY'S WATCHING!
Tom Wilson